EB-3 Consular Processing

Getting the Green Card at the Consulate by an employment petition

Attorney Brian D. Lerner

LAW OFFICES OF BRIAN D. LERNER
A PROFESSIONAL CORPORATION

ATTORNEY DRAFTED IMMIGRATION PETITIONS

By

Brian D. Lerner

Attorney at Law

Disclaimer and Terms of Use:

INTRODUCTION

There are a multitude of different immigration petitions and applications. They are complex and full of requirements. Obviously, it would be best to hire an immigration attorney to best prepare the petitions and applications. However, this can certainly cost thousands of dollars.

The next best option is to get a sample of the petition written by an experienced immigration attorney. The samples cost a fraction what would be charged by an immigration attorney. However, while the reader has to alter, amend and change the parts of the sample petition to reflect their actual situation, it is a fantastic roadmap for them to use. If the reader has purchased the entire petition or application, they will have real live samples of cover letters, forms, declarations, affidavits and the necessary exhibits to use. The samples come from real cases and the names of those clients have been redacted to protect the privacy of that person or corporation.

These are petitions and applications that have been drafted by an experienced immigration attorney with over 25 years of experience. Get the benefits of that experience without the costs.

CONTENTS

About the Law Offices of Brian D. Lerner

Brian D. Lerner has been a licensed attorney since 1992 and started the Law Offices of Brian D. Lerner, APC. The law practice consists of Immigration and Nationality Law and everything involved with and regarding immigration which includes citizenship, investment visas, family and employment visas, removal and deportation hearings, appeals, waivers, adjustment, consulate processing and all types of immigration and citizenship matters. Thousands of families have been reunited and/or permitted to stay in the U.S. and/or return to the U.S. because of the successful work of Immigration Attorney Brian D. Lerner.

This law offices handles all types of immigration cases including family based and employment based. Immigration issues range from immigration court proceedings to trying to fix what paralegals may have done that was neither correct nor proper. Foreign nationals must have experience lawyers admitted to practice law.

The Law Offices of Brian D. Lerner, APC, handles cases arising from business visas, work permits, Green Cards, non-immigrant visas, deportation, citizenship, appeals and all areas of immigration. The Law Offices of Brian D. Lerner, APC does EB-5 Investor Visas, H-1B Specialty Occupation, L-1 Intracompany Transferee, E-2 Treaty Investor, E-1 Treaty Trader, O-1 Extraordinary Ability among others. Regarding immigrant visas for the Green Card, the firm does PERM and advanced degree PERM, Family Petitions, and Extraordinary Alien Petitions. In addition to affirmative petitions, the Law Firm represents people in people in deportation and removal hearings, including political asylum, withholding of removal, and convention against torture cases.

Brian D. Lerner has been certified as an expert in Immigration & Nationality Law by the California State Bar, Board of Legal Specialization since 2000 and has been re-certified three times. He now passes on his decades of experience by allowing the Reader, Law Schools, Professors and other Immigration Attorneys to purchase sample petitions on every facet of Immigration Law.

About the EB-3 Consular Processing Visa

The EB-3 CP is an Employment-Based Visa which is for skilled workers, professionals, and other workers. After the PERM is approved, assuming you have an employer sponsoring you and either a couple years of experience or a bachelor's degree, the EB-3 is for you.

ATTORNEY COVER LETTER

Law Offices of Brian D. Lerner

A PROFESSIONAL CORPORATION

CERTIFIED SPECIALIST IN IMMIGRATION AND NATIONALITY LAW
ADMITTED TO THE U.S. SUPREME COURT

LONG BEACH, CALIFORNIA
(562) 495-0554
CARSON, CALIFORNIA
(310) 684-3470

September 7, 2018

National Visa Center
Attn: DR
31 Rochester Avenue, Suite 100
Portsmouth, NH 03801-2914

      Re: **Application for U.S. Immigrant Visa**
           Petitioner: Consultants for America's Veterans, LLC / ███████████
           Beneficiary: ████████████
           NVC Case Number: ████████████

Dear Sir/Madam:

We hereby submit the following in support of ███████████ (hereinafter as "Applicant") Immigrant Visa application. The required Immigrant Visa Fee has been paid electronically (see Exhibit "6") and the DS-260, Immigrant Visa Electronic Application, has also been submitted electronically (see Exhibit "7").

Enclosed please find the following documents:

Exhibits

Exhibit:	Description:
"1"	Applicant's Birth Certificate;
"2"	Applicant's Foreign Passport;
"3"	Applicant's Military Records;
"4"	Applicant's Resume;
"5"	Applicant's High School Diploma with English Translation;
"6"	Proof of Payment of Immigrant Visa Fee;
"7"	Confirmation of Form DS-260, Immigrant Visa Electronic Application;
"8"	I-140 Approval Notice; and
"9"	Petitioner's 2016 and 2017 Income Tax Return.

Please note that Applicant has requested her Criminal Information Certificate (confiration number 325291) however, according to the U.S. Visa: Reciprocity and Civil Document by Country page, the certificate will be sent directly to the Consular Section.

Based on the foregoing, we believe that the NVC has everything necessary to forward the instant application to the U.S. Consulate for final processing. Thank you for your consideration in this matter

Should you have any further questions, please feel free to contact our office at (562) 495-0554.

Sincerely,

Brian D. Lerner
Attorney at Law

EXHIBITS

EXHIBIT '1'

Applicant's Birth Certificate

מדינת ישראל
دولة اسرائيل
STATE OF ISRAEL

תעודת לידה
BIRTH CERTIFICATE

Surname		ישראלי	שם המשפחה
Given name		מרסל	השם הפרטי
Given name of father		יעקב	השם הפרטי של האב
Given name of mother		זהבה	השם הפרטי של האם

Surname of mother's father		עוזר	שם המשפחה של אבי האם
Identity no.	0 2178242 0		מספר זהות
Sex	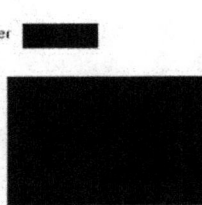	נקבה	המין
Nationality		יהודי	הלאום
Religion		יהודי	הדת
Place of birth		תל אביב - יפו	מקום הלידה
Hospital's name		בית היולדות	שם בית החולים
Date of birth	7 May 1983	7 במאי 1983	תאריך הלידה

I hereby certify that the above newborn is listed in the Births Register.

This certificate is issued in accordance with article 30 of the Population Registry Law of 1965
Ministry of Foreign Affairs in Jerusalem Authority

Date 13 October 2013

הנני מאשר כי הילוד נרשם בספר הלידות

התעודה ניתנה בהתאם לסעיף 30
לחוק מרשם האוכלוסין תשכ"ה - 1965
במשרד החוץ בירושלים

בתאריך 13 באוקטובר 2013

Seal of Ministry   Name and Signature of registrar

לכבוד

ישראלי	מרסל
135	הרצל
6810104	תל אביב - יפו

APOSTILLE
(Convention de La Haye du 5 octobre 1961)

1	STATE OF ISRAEL		מדינת ישראל	1
2	THIS PUBLIC DOCUMENT HAS BEEN SIGNED BY MR./MS	בן-שמעון אורית BEN-SHIMON ORIT	מסמך ציבורי זה נחתם בידי מר/גב'	2
3	ACTING IN THE CAPACITY OF HEAD OF DOCUMENTATION BRANCH		המכהן בתואר ר' ענף תיעוד	3
4	BEARS THE SEAL/STAMP OF THE MINISTRY OF	משרד החוץ FOREIGN AFFAIRS	ונושא את החותם/חותמת של	4
5	CERTIFIED AT THE MINISTRY OF FOREIGN AFFAIRS		אושר במשרד החוץ	5
6	THE	14/10/2013	ביום	6
7	BY		על ידי	7
8	NO 702511		מס' 702511	8
9	SEAL/STAMP		חותם/חותמת	9
10	SIGNATURE JERUSALEM		חתימה ירושלים	10

EXHIBIT '2'

Applicant's Foreign Passport

[redacted]

PASSPORT דרכון STATE OF ISRAEL מדינת ישראל

Type / סוג
P / ד

Code of State / סמל המדינה
ISR

Passport No. / מס' דרכון
20889488

Surname
[redacted]

שם משפחה
ישראלי

Given name
[redacted]

שם פרטי
מרסל

Nationality
ISRAELI

אזרחות
ישראלית

Date of birth / תאריך לידה
07/05/1983

I.D. No. / מס' זהות
0-2178242-0

Sex / מין
F / נ

Place of birth
ISRAEL

מקום לידה
ישראל

Date of issue / תאריך הוצאת
08/08/2013

Date of expiry / תאריך פקיעת תוקף
07/08/2023

Authority - I.C. Passport at-
LOS ANGELES

סמכות - ממונת דרכונים ב-
לוס אנג'לס

```
P<ISRISRAELI<<MARCELLE<<<<<<<<<<<<<<<<<<<<<<<
20889488<9ISR8305077F23080760<2178242<0<<<64
```

EXHIBIT '3'

Applicant's Military Records

Form no. 6

Serial No. 177/18

CERTIFICATION OF TRANSLATION

I the undersigned , ████████████
(full name)

Notary at 37 Sderot Shaul Hamelech, Tel - Aviv
hereby declare that I am well acquainted with the
Hebrew and English languages and that the document
attached to this certification
marked A is a correct
(letter or number)

translation into English
(language of translation)

of ☐ the original document / ☐ certified copy of the
original document / ☒ a document that is not the
original document nor a certified copy of the original
document*

drawn up in the Hebrew
language, which has been produced to me, and ☐ is
also attached herewith/ ☒ a photocopy of which is
also attached herewith** and marked B
(letter or number)

In witness whereof I certify the correctness of the said
translation by my signature and seal.

This day September 3rd, 2018

Fees paid: 434 NIS including VAT

_____
Notary's Seal and Signature

*mark the appropriate option; if marked "a document that is
not original document nor a certified copy of the original
document", you may indicate that the document was
received by facsimile or that it is an uncertified photocopy
of a document or a similar indication.

** marked the appropriate option.

אישור תרגום

טופס מס' 6

מס' סידורי 177/18

אני החתים גודי קרמרמן
(שם מלא)

נוטריונית ב - שדרות שאול המלך 37, תל - אביב מצהירה
בזה. כי אני שילטת היטב בשפות העברית ו - האנגלית וכי
המסמך המצורף

△ לאישור זה והמסומן
(באות או במספר)

הוא תרגום מדויק ל אנגלית
(שפת התרגום)

של ☐ המסמך המקורי / ☐ העתק מאושר של המסמך
המקורי / ☒ מסמך שאינו המסמך המקורי או העתק
מאושר שלו

שנערך בשפה העברית שהוצג לפני
ואשר ☐ הוא / ☒ העתק צילומי שלו ** מצורף גם
הוא לאישורי זה והמסומן B
(באות או במספר)

להראות אני מאשרת את דיוק התרגום האמור בחתימתי
ובחותמי.

03/09/2018

שי בסך 434 ש"ח כולל מע"מ שולם

נוטריונית/וחתימתי

מסמך זה ונוסח ע"י מחוקל הנוטסטים של אסקי • ההוצאה לאור טל' 03-6242060, פקס 03-6240805

A'

Logo. Computerized document digitally signed and certified by a Certification Authority cosign.

Unclassified

OFFICIAL CERTIFICATE

ISRAELI DEFENSE FORCES
PUBLIC INQIRIES OFFICER
A.P.S.   02099
TELEPHONE: 1111
28th DAY OF   TAMUZ 5778
JULY   11th   2018

To whom it may concern

Re: Certification of evaluation certificate's contents for the discharged soldier from mandatory military service –
True copy

1. I hereby certify that this is a copy of the evaluation certificate's contents for the discharged soldier

Personal number	Rank	Surname	Given name	ID number

At the time of discharge from the I.D.F. The original certificate is produced and delivered to the soldier at the time of discharge by the discharge department at the human resources division.

Discharge date: 08/02/2004   Commander's evaluation:
Discharge rank: First Lieutenant   Serious
Soldier's behavior: Remarkable   Responsible
Service period: **Mandatory** 01 years & 09 months   Personal high level
                Regular 07 months   Well-developed critique capability
Discharge reason: Completion of regular service.   Friendly
Rifleman: 02   Popular among her friends

Military professions acquired

Profession's name	Type	Parallel civil	Type
Communications Officer			
Small computer operator	06		

2. This certificate is a copy of the evaluation certificate form (F 807).

(--------------)

_____ Lieutenant colonel

Public Inquiries Officer

The certificate uses masculine form but is intended for both genders
UNCLASSIFIED

מיועתק

אישור רשמי

B'

צבא	ההגנה	
קצינת	פניות	
דייצ		
טלפון :		
כ"ח	בתמוז	התשע"ח
11	ביולי	2018

לכל מאן דבעי

הנדון: אישור על תוכן תעודת הערכה לחייל המשתחרר משירות סדיר – העתק נאמן למקור

1. הריני לאשר כי זהו העתק תוכנה של תעודת ההערכה לחייל המשתחרר

| 021782420 | מרסל | ישראלי | סגן | 7217676 |
| מספר זהות | שם פרטי | שם משפחה | דרגה | מספר אישי |

בעת שחרורו מצה"ל. התעודה המקורית מופקת ונמסרת לחייל במעמד השחרור על ידי מדור השחרורים שבאגף כוח האדם.

הערכת המפקד		**תאריך השחרור:** 08/02/2004
רצינית		**דרגת השיחרור:** סגן
אחראית		**התנהגות החייל:** ראויה לציון
בעלת רמה אישית גבוהה		**משך השירות:** חובה 01 שנים ו- 09 חדשים
בעלת כושר ביקורת מפותח		קבע 07 חדשים
חברותית		**סיבת השחרור:** תום שירות קבע
מקובלת על חבריה		**רובאי:** 02

מקצועות צבאיים שנרכשו

שם המקצוע	סוג	אזרחי מקביל	סוג
קצין קשר			
מפעיל מחשב קטן	06		

2. אישור זה מהווה העתק לטופס תעודת הערכה (ט' 807).

דנה זרקו מודריק,
קצינת פניות

סגן אלוף
הציבור

'האישור מנוסח בלשון זכר אולם מיועד לשני המינים

13 | P a g e

Form no. 6

Serial No. 178/18

CERTIFICATION OF TRANSLATION

I the undersigned ██████████
(full name)

Notary at 37 Sderot Shaul Hamelech, Tel - Aviv
hereby declare that I am well acquainted with the
Hebrew and English languages and that the document
attached to this certification
marked A is a correct
(letter or number)

translation into English
(language of translation)

of ☒ the original document / ☐ certified copy of the
original document / ☐ a document that is not the
original document nor a certified copy of the original
document*

drawn up in the Hebrew
language, which has been produced to me, and ☐ is
also attached herewith/ ☒ a photocopy of which is
also attached herewith** and marked B
(letter or number)

In witness whereof I certify the correctness of the said
translation by my signature and seal.

This day September 6th, 2018

Fees paid: 434 NIS including VATF

Notary's Seal

*mark the appropriate option; if marked "a document that is
not original document nor a certified copy of the original
document", you may indicate that the document was
received by facsimile or that it is an uncertified photocopy
of a document or a similar indication.

** marked the appropriate option.

טופס מס' 6

מס' סידורי 178/18

אישור תרגום

אני הח"מ ג'ודי קרמרמן
(השם המלא)

נוטריון ב - שדרות שאול המלך 37, תל - אביב מצהיר
בזה, כי אני שולט היטב בשמות העברית ו - האנגלית וכי
המסמך המצורף A
לאישור זה והמסומן (באות או במספר)

הוא תרגום מדוייק ל אנגלית
(שפת התרגום)

של ☒ המסמך המקורי / ☐ העתק מאושר של המסמך
המקורי / ☐ מסמך שאינו המסמך המקורי או העתק
מאושר שלו

הערוך בשפה העברית שהוצג לפני
ואשר ☐ הוא/ ☒ העתק צילומי שלו ** מצורף גם
הוא לאישורי זה ומסומן B
(באות או במספר)

ולראיה אני מאשר את דיוק התרגום האמור בחתימת ידי
ובחותמי.

יום 06/09/2018

רי בסך 434 ש"ח כולל מע"מ שנגבם

את התלופה השתאימה; צוין ימסמך שאינו המסמך
או העתק מאושר שלי
ציין לצדו אם נקבל בפקסימיליה או שהוא צילום
של מסמך וכדומה

ה תמתאימה.

משמך זה הוכן ע"י מחולל הטפסים של אסקי - ההובאה לאור טל 03-6242060, 03-6240603 פקס

ISRAELI DEFENSE FORCES

EVALUATION CERTIFICATE

FOR THE DISCHARGED SOLDIER
FROM MILITARY SERVICE

F 807 number (02-01) 441108613

A'

Personal number		Rank	First Lieutenant	Surname		Given name		February 8th, 2004	021782420
						Reason of discharge	Discharge date		ID number
							End of regular service		

Service type	Service Length	02 Years	04 Months

*Military professions acquired		Officer	01
	Profession name		Type

Awards, decorations and citations

Evaluation	Dedicated
Responsible	
High personal level	
Well-developed critique capability	
Friendly	
Popular among her friends	

Special remarks

4565789	Major
P.N.	Rank

Stamp: Israel Defense Forces Discharge Dept.

Behavior
(In mandatory service only)

Behavior Scale:
Very good, Almost Very Good, Good,
Almost Good, Satisfactory, Non-
satisfactory

(-------------------)	Given name	Surname
Signature	February 8th, 2004	
	Date	

* Profession list does not express the medical competence for the profession.
F 807 number (02-01) 441108613

NOTAIRE
ג'ודי
קרמרמן
NOTARY

16 | P a g e

B′

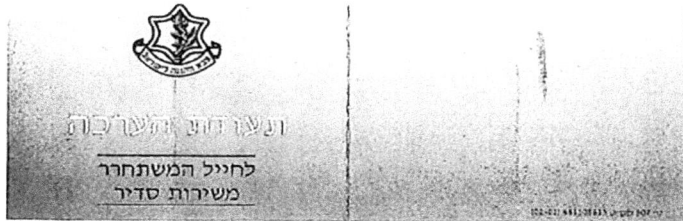

ו.ע.ל.ד.ות ה.ע.ר.כ.ת

לחייל המשתחרר
משירות סדיר

EXHIBIT '4'

Applicant's Resume

EXHIBIT '4'

Applicant's Resume

Marcelle Israeli

Summary of qualifications

Highly qualified and detail-oriented professional. Have excellent communication skills, demonstrated by over 10 years of experience in costumer relations and team collaborations. Have the abilities to adapt into different environments rapidly. Forward thinking with identifying problems and giving efficient solutions.

Experience

2012- Current: Consulate General of Israel , Los Angeles, California

Consular Department: assisting Israeli citizens to obtain passport / documentations from Israeli officials. Examining and providing visas and other various services, to non- citizens who wish to work/ study/ travel to Israel. Accompany and supporting the clients throughout the wholes process and maintain professional customer relations.

2008-2012: El-Al Israeli Airlines , Tel Aviv Israel

Flight attendant: customer service at the business department. Working in different aircrafts, with various teams. Providing services and safety in a limited time-frame and different environments.

2006-2007: Electra Real Estate, Tel Aviv, Israel

CEO Secretary: Administrative operations and managing the CEO department at one of the leading real estate companies in Israel. That traded at the Tel Aviv Stock- Exchange.

2004-2006: David Intercontinental Hotel, Tel Aviv , Israel

Guest Relations Department: responsible for VIP guest service. Planning VIP events as well as VIP customer retention and distribution of the hotel chain membership.

2004: Impact Company Tel Aviv, Israel

Ground Hostess: Hosting special events, conventions and exhibitions.

2001-2004: Israeli Defense Force, Tel Aviv, Israel

Officer: at the Communication and Computer Forces. Served at a secret electronic-warfare unit. Military rank: First Lieutenant.

Skills

Independent, Organized, representative, very responsible dedicated and loyal. As well as creative and initiative minded.

Applicant's High School Diploma with English Translation

Form no. 6

Serial No. 476/17

CERTIFICATION OF TRANSLATION

I the undersigned , ██████████████
(full name)

Notary at 37 Sderot Shaul Hamelech, Tel - Aviv hereby declare that I am well acquainted with the Hebrew and English languages and that the document attached to this certification
marked A is a correct
(letter or number)

translation into English
(language of translation)

of ⊠ the original document / ☐ certified copy of the original document / ☐ a document that is not the original document nor a certified copy of the original document*

drawn up in the Hebrew
language, which has been produced to me, and ☐ is also attached herewith/ ⊠ a photocopy of which is also attached herewith** and marked B
(letter or number)

In witness whereof I certify the correctness of the said translation by my signature and seal.

This day October 31st, 2017

Fees paid: 433 NIS including VAT

_S. K_____
Notary's Seal and Signature

*mark the appropriate option; if marked "a document that is not original document nor a certified copy of the original document", you may indicate that the document was received by facsimile or that it is an uncertified photocopy of a document or a similar indication.

** marked the appropriate option.

טופס מספר 6

מס׳ סידורי 476/17

אישור תרגום

אני החתים גידי קרמרמן
(שם החתום)

נוטריון ב - שדרות שאול המלך 37, תל - אביב מצהירה בזאת, כי אני שולטת היטב בשמות העברית ו - האנגלית וכי המסמך המצורף

לאישור זה והמסומן A
(מאות או בספרה)

הוא תרגום נוטריון ל אנגלית
(שפת התרגום)

של ⊠ המסמך המקורי / ☐ העתק מאושר של המסמך המקורי / ☐ מסמך שאינו המסמך המקורי או העתק מאושר שלו

הערוך בשפה העברית שהוצג לגני

אשר ☐ הוא/ ⊠ העתק צילומי שלו ** מצורף גם הוא לאישור זה ומסומן B
(באות או בספרה)

ראיה אני מאשרת את דיוק התרגום האמור בחתימת ובחותמי.

31/10/2017

סך 433 שייח כולל מע״מ שולם.

זה העתק ע״י בחולל הנוטריון של אסקי - הרוצרבה לטור טל 03 6242050, 6242060, פקס 6240501-03

A'

Israel
Ministry of Education, Culture & Sports
"Ramot" Municipal High School

Bat Yam

MATRICULATION CERTIFICATE

The matriculate ▊▊▊▊▊▊   I.D. Number ▊▊▊▊

Completed her studies at school in the year of 5761 (2001)

Major --------------Major ++++++++++++++++++++++++++++

Passed the exams of the Ministry of Education in the following subjects and achieved these grades:

Subject	Study Units	Grade
Bible	2	Good...........................78
Hebrew Expression	2	Very Good....................88
Literature	2	Good...........................84
English	5	Good...........................84
Mathematics	5	Good...........................83
Chemistry	5	Good...........................75
History	2	Almost Good.................70
Computer Science	3	Excellent.......................97
Civics	1	Almost Good.................74

Score grading:

Excellent (10) 95 to 100; Very Good (9) 85 to 94; Good (8) 75 to 84; Almost Good (7) 65 to 74; Sufficient (6) 55 to 64; Barely Sufficient (5) 45 to 54; Non Sufficient (4) 05 to 44;

School symbol 540492

1745

"Ramot" Municipal High School

███████████

School's administration hereby confirms that

The matriculate ███████████ I.D. Number ███████████

Completed her studies at school in the additional subjects as follows and achieved the following final grades:

Subject	Study Units	Grade	
Physics	1	Very Good	(94)
Biology	1	Very Good	(86)
Physical Education	2	Very Good	(85)

This part of the certificate is printed within the school

Based on the matriculate's studies, achievements at school and matriculate exams, this matriculation certificate is issued to the matriculate, granting her to be accepted to studies in high education institutions and education employee training, subject to their customary acceptance terms.

(-------------------)   (-------------------)

Headmaster's signature and school's stamp   Ministry of Education

Stamp: Bat Yam Municipality - "Ramot" Municipal High School

Jerusalem

11th day of Adar 5764
March 4th, 2004

806854

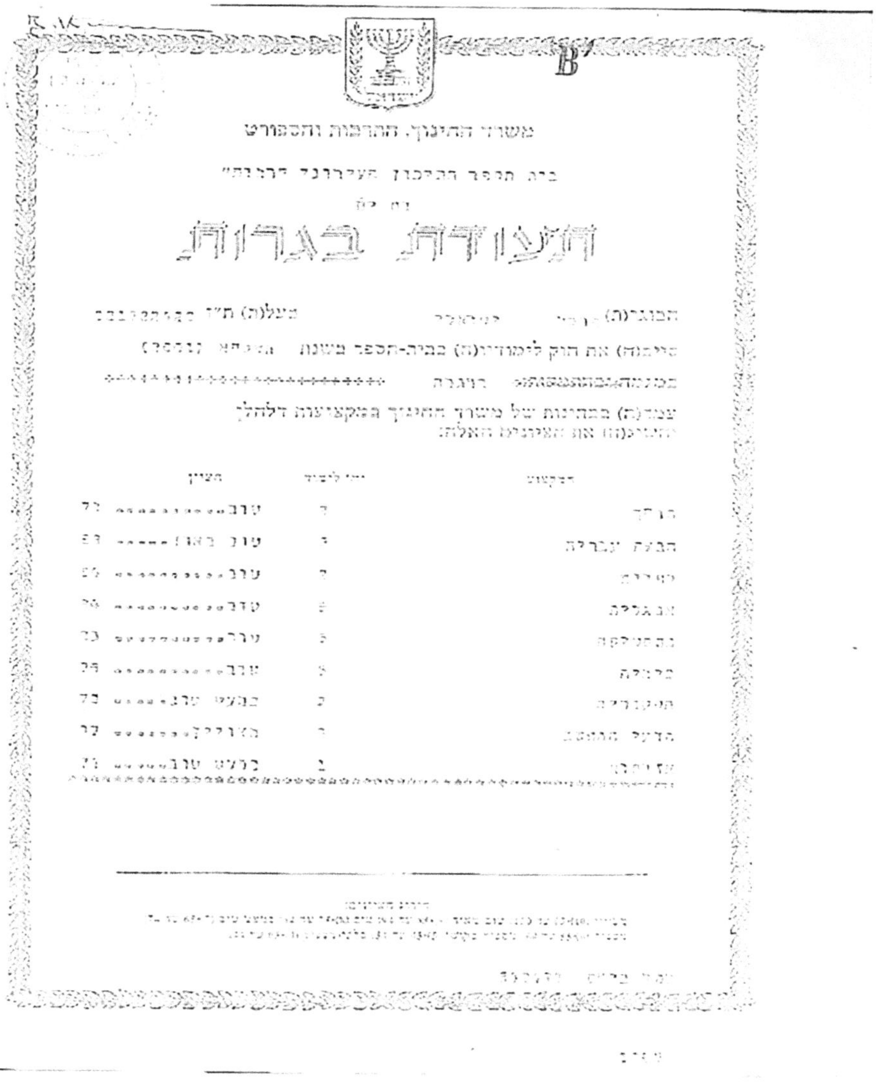

B'

משרד החינוך, התרבות והספורט

בית הספר התיכון העירוני דרגה"

על שם

תעודת בגרות

הבוגר(ת) _____ ן רה _____ ילידי/ד _____ מעלות(ה) ת"ז _____

סיימה(ה) את חוק לימודיו(ה) בבית-הספר בשנות _____

מכינה _____ דוגברה

עמד(ה) בבחינות של משרד החינוך במקציעות דלהלן

המקצוע	יח"ל לימוד	הציון
תנ"ך	ד	עובר
הבעה עברית	ד	עובר
ספרות	ד	עובר
אנגלית	5	עובר
מתמטיקה	5	עובר
מולדת	5	עובר
היסטוריה	5	עובר
חינוך גופני	5	עובר
אזרחות	1	עובר

הערות כלליות

מנהל בית-הספר _____

25 | P a g e

EXHIBIT '6'

Proof of Payment of Immigrant Visa Fee

EXHIBIT '6'

Proof of Payment of Immigrant Visa Fee

Payment Receipts for IV Case JRS2018735008
IV Fee Payment Receipt Details

Principal Applicant ▇▇▇▇▇▇▇▇▇▇▇
Payment of Services Initiated 27-AUG-2018 18:04:02
Payment Processed Date 28-AUG-2018
Payment Amount $345.00
Payer ▇▇▇▇▇▇
Payer Email ▇▇▇▇▇▇▇▇▇▇▇
Transaction ID 26BSBVUJ

Applicant	IV Fee Payment Status	Fee Amount
▇▇▇▇▇▇▇▇▇	PAID	$345.00

Next Steps

If your payment status shows that it is IN PROCESS, wait two to three business days for the payment to clear. Then sign into the system again to check for a status update.

If your payment status shows a status other than IN PROCESS or PAID, sign in to the Immigrant Visa Invoice Payment Center page https://ceac.state.gov/CTRAC/Invoice/Signon.aspx and click on Get Help.

If you receive a notice that your case has entered termination, **do not attempt to pay any fees**. You must contact the National Visa Center (NVC) immediately to resume processing of your petition. You can find NVC contact information at nvc.state.gov/ask

When the IV fee payment status is PAID:

1. Each applicant must complete and submit an Online Immigrant Visa and Alien Registration Application (DS-260). To submit your application, go to http://ceac.state.gov/iv, and sign in. Read the Summary Information. Click on the IV APPLICATION tab and follow the application instructions.
2. To review specific U.S. Embassy or Consulate instructions and options that may apply to your case, go to nvc.state.gov/document. You will find the information in a downloadable PDF format at the bottom of the page.
3. To complete your Immigrant Visa Application, you must submit copies of all supporting documents. Go to nvc.state.gov/submit. You will find instructions if you are required to email your documents, as well as the processing and mailing information.
4. If you are required to submit physical copies of your documents, you must include a barcoded cover sheet to identify your documents.

- If you received an Instruction Packet from the NVC, it contains a cover sheet. You can send that cover sheet or a copy of the cover sheet.
- If you need a new cover sheet, print one by clicking the Print Document Cover Sheet button on the Receipt page.
- If you cannot print a cover sheet, click the Email Document Cover Sheet button. Then send an electronic copy to an email address where you can print it.

IMPORTANT NOTES:

- If you decide to file Form I-601A, Application for Provisional Unlawful Presence Waiver with USCIS, you must include a copy of this fee payment receipt or USCIS will reject your Form I-601A.
- Please keep this receipt for your records. If you can't print the receipt now, return to the Receipt Screen and email a copy to an address where you can print it later.
- Do not let more than one-year pass without contacting the NVC about your immigrant visa petition. If a period of one-year passes from the last date of contact, all submitted forms and fees will expire and you must resubmit them to resume processing.
- You will find the next steps about AOS fee payments on the AOS fee payment receipt.

EXHIBIT '7'

Confirmation of Form DS-260, Immigrant Visa Electronic Application

Online Immigrant Visa and Alien Registration Application (DS-260)

Immigrant Visa and Alien Registration Application Confirmation

Thank You

You have successfully submitted an Immigrant Visa and Alien Registration Application (Form DS-260). You must bring to your visa interview proof that you submitted this form by printing a confirmation page using the below button. Do not print a copy of this screen; use the below PRINT CONFIRMATION button to print a page with a unique barcode related to your visa application. You can print a confirmation from this website at any time.

Next Step

Your Immigrant Visa and Alien Registration Application (Form DS-260) was sent to the National Visa Center (NVC) for review. **However, NVC will not review your Form DS-260 until they have received the required financial and civil documents that you must also submit.** If you have not sent NVC those items, please do so now. Visit http://nvc.state.gov (English) or http://nvc.state.gov/espanol (Spanish) and review Steps 4-6 for instructions.

NVC will review your DS-260 IV application, financial, and civil documents upon receipt of all documents. If the documents you submitted are insufficient or incomplete, NVC will send instructions on how to correct your submission. NVC cannot schedule your visa interview until your supporting documentation is complete.

Your Visa Interview

Once you have a visa interview appointment, you need to:

1. Obtain and submit photographs that meet the Department of State's visa requirements.
2. Review the information for the U.S. Embassy where your visa interview will occur.

Please use the buttons below for information on these items as well as instructions for submitting documents to NVC.

During the interview with a consular officer, you will be required to sign your application by providing a "biometric signature" – in other words, your fingerprints. By providing this biometric signature, you are certifying under penalty of perjury that you have read and understood the questions in your immigrant visa application. You are also certifying that all statements that appear in your immigrant visa application have been made by you and are true and complete to the best of your knowledge and belief. At the time of your interview, you will also be required to certify under penalty of perjury that all statements in your application and those made during your interview are true and complete to the best of your knowledge and belief.

This confirms the submission of the Immigrant Visa and Alien Registration application for:

Name Provided:
Country/Region of Origin
(Nationality):
Completed On:
Case No:
Confirmation No:

JRS2018735008

THIS IS NOT A VISA

AA0089SDII

Version 01.02.00

EXHIBIT '8'

I-140 Approval Notice

Receipt Number LIN1818050752		Case Type
Received Date 06/18/2018	Priority Date 10/23/2017	Petitioner
Notice Date 07/02/2018	Page 1 of 1	Beneficiary

c/o BRIAN DAVID LERNER
LAW OFFICE BRIAN D LERNER
3233 E BROADWAY
LONG BEACH CA 90803

Notice Type: Approval Notice
Section: Skilled Worker, Sec 203(b)(3)(A)(i)
Consulate: NVC
ETA Case Number: A17296011835
SOC Code: 273031

The above petition has been approved. We have sent it to the Department of State National Visa Center (NVC), 32 Rochester Avenue, Portsmouth, NH 03801-2909. NVC processes all approved immigrant visa petitions that need consular action. It also determines which consular post is the appropriate consulate to complete visa processing. The NVC will then forward the approved petition to that consulate.

This completes all USCIS action on this petition. You should allow a minimum of 30 days for Department of State processing before contacting the NVC. If you have not received any correspondence from the NVC within 30 days, you may contact the NVC by e-mail at NVCINQUIRY@state.gov. You will need to enter the USCIS receipt number from this approval notice in the subject line. In order to receive information about your petition, you will need to include the Petitioner's name and date of birth, and the Applicant's name and date of birth, in the body of the e-mail.

The NVC will contact the person for whom you are petitioning concerning further immigrant visa processing steps.

The approval of this visa petition does not in itself grant any immigration status and does not guarantee that the alien beneficiary will subsequently be found to be eligible for a visa, for admission to the United States, or for an extension, change, or adjustment of status.

THIS FORM IS NOT A VISA AND MAY NOT BE USED IN PLACE OF A VISA.

The Small Business Regulatory Enforcement and Fairness Act established the Office of the National Ombudsman (ONO) at the Small Business Administration. The ONO assists small businesses with issues related to federal regulations. If you are a small business with a comment or complaint about regulatory enforcement, you may contact the ONO at www.sba.gov/ombudsman or phone 202-205-2417 or fax 202-481-5719.

NOTICE: Although this application or petition has been approved, USCIS and the U.S. Department of Homeland Security reserve the right to verify this information before and/or after making a decision on your case so we can ensure that you have complied with applicable laws, rules, regulations, and other legal authorities. We may review public information and records, contact others by mail, the internet or phone, conduct site inspections of businesses and residences, or use other methods of verification. We will use the information obtained to determine whether you are eligible for the benefit you seek. If we find any derogatory information, we will follow the law in determining whether to provide you (and the legal representative listed on your Form G-28, if you submitted one) an opportunity to address that information before we make a formal decision on your case or start proceedings.

Please see the additional information on the back. You will be notified separately about any other cases you filed.

Nebraska Service Center
U. S. CITIZENSHIP & IMMIGRATION SVC
P.O. Box 82521
Lincoln NE 68501-2521

USCIS Contact Center: 1-800-375-5283

EXHIBIT '9'

Petitioner's 2016 and 2017 Income Tax Return

1040 Department of the Treasury—Internal Revenue Service (99)
U.S. Individual Income Tax Return | 2016 | OMB No. 1545-0074 | IRS Use Only—Do not write or staple in this space.

For the year Jan. 1–Dec. 31, 2016, or other tax year beginning , 2016, ending , 20 | See separate instructions.

Your first name and initial	Last name		Your social security number
▮▮▮	▮▮▮		
If a joint return, spouse's first name and initial	Last name		Spouse's social security number

Home address (number and street). If you have a P.O. box, see instructions. ▮▮▮ | Apt. no. ▮

City, town or post office, state, and ZIP code. If you have a foreign address, also complete spaces below (see instructions).

Foreign country name | Foreign province/state/county | Foreign postal code

A Make sure the SSN(s) above and on line 6c are correct.

Presidential Election Campaign
Check here if you, or your spouse if filing jointly, want $3 to go to this fund. Checking a box below will not change your tax or refund. ☐ You ☐ Spouse

Filing Status
Check only one box

1. ☒ Single
2. ☐ Married filing jointly (even if only one had income)
3. ☐ Married filing separately. Enter spouse's SSN above and full name here ▶
4. ☐ Head of household (with qualifying person). (See instructions.) If the qualifying person is a child but not your dependent, enter this child's name here ▶
5. ☐ Qualifying widow(er) with dependent child

Exemptions

6a. ☒ Yourself. If someone can claim you as a dependent, do not check box 6a
b. ☐ Spouse
} Boxes checked on 6a and 6b **1**

c. Dependents:

(1) First name Last name	(2) Dependent's social security number	(3) Dependent's relationship to you	(4) ✓ if child under age 17 qualifying for child tax credit (see instructions)
▮▮▮	▮▮▮	▮▮▮	

If more than four dependents, see instructions and check here ▶ ☐

No. of children on 6c who:
• lived with you
• did not live with you due to divorce or separation (see instructions)

Dependents on 6c not entered above **1**

Add numbers on lines above ▶ **2**

d. Total number of exemptions claimed

Income

Attach Form(s) W-2 here. Also attach Forms W-2G and 1099-R if tax was withheld.

If you did not get a W-2, see instructions.

7	Wages, salaries, tips, etc. Attach Form(s) W-2	7	48,311
8a	Taxable interest. Attach Schedule B if required	8a	
b	Tax-exempt interest. Do not include on line 8a	8b	
9a	Ordinary dividends. Attach Schedule B if required	9a	
b	Qualified dividends	9b	
10	Taxable refunds, credits, or offsets of state and local income taxes	10	
11	Alimony received	11	
12	Business income or (loss). Attach Schedule C or C-EZ	12	70,083
13	Capital gain or (loss). Attach Schedule D if required. If not required, check here ▶ ☐	13	
14	Other gains or (losses). Attach Form 4797	14	
15a	IRA distributions 15a	b Taxable amount	15b	
16a	Pensions and annuities 16a	b Taxable amount	16b	
17	Rental real estate, royalties, partnerships, S corporations, trusts, etc. Attach Schedule E	17	
18	Farm income or (loss). Attach Schedule F	18	
19	Unemployment compensation	19	
20a	Social security benefits 20a	b Taxable amount	20b	
21	Other income. List type and amount TOTAL DEBT CANCELED	21	14,487
22	Combine the amounts in the far right column for lines 7 through 21. This is your total income ▶	22	132,881

Adjusted Gross Income

23	Educator expenses	23		
24	Certain business expenses of reservists, performing artists, and fee-basis government officials. Attach Form 2106 or 2106-EZ	24		
25	Health savings account deduction. Attach Form 8889	25		
26	Moving expenses. Attach Form 3903	26		
27	Deductible part of self-employment tax. Attach Schedule SE	27	4,951	
28	Self-employed SEP, SIMPLE, and qualified plans	28		
29	Self-employed health insurance deduction	29		
30	Penalty on early withdrawal of savings	30		
31a	Alimony paid b Recipient's SSN ▶	31a		
32	IRA deduction	32		
33	Student loan interest deduction	33		
34	Tuition and fees. Attach Form 8917	34		
35	Domestic production activities deduction. Attach Form 8903	35		
36	Add lines 23 through 35		36	4,951
37	Subtract line 36 from line 22. This is your adjusted gross income ▶		37	127,930

For Disclosure, Privacy Act, and Paperwork Reduction Act Notice, see separate instructions.
DAA

Form **1040** (2016)

Tax and Credits	38	Amount from line 37 (adjusted gross income)		38	127,930
	39a	Check if: { You were born before January 2, 1952, ☐ Blind. Spouse was born before January 2, 1952, ☐ Blind. } Total boxes checked ► 39a ☐			
Standard Deduction for—	b	If your spouse itemizes on a separate return or you were a dual-status alien, check here ► 39b ☐			
	40	Itemized deductions (from Schedule A) or your standard deduction (see left margin)		40	6,300
• People who check any box on line 39a or 39b or who can be claimed as a dependent, see instructions.	41	Subtract line 40 from line 38		41	121,630
	42	Exemptions. If line 38 is $155,650 or less, multiply $4,050 by the number on line 6d. Otherwise, see instructions		42	8,100
	43	Taxable income. Subtract line 42 from line 41. If line 42 is more than line 41, enter -0-		43	113,530
• All others:	44	Tax (see instr.). Check if any from: a ☐ Form(s) 8814 b ☐ Form 4972 c ☐		44	24,825
Single or Married filing separately, $6,300	45	Alternative minimum tax (see instructions). Attach Form 6251		45	
Married filing jointly or Qualifying widow(er), $12,600	46	Excess advance premium tax credit repayment. Attach Form 8962		46	
Head of household, $9,300	47	Add lines 44, 45, and 46	►	47	24,825
	48	Foreign tax credit. Attach Form 1116 if required	48		
	49	Credit for child and dependent care expenses. Attach Form 2441	49		
	50	Education credits from Form 8863, line 19	50		
	51	Retirement savings contributions credit. Attach Form 8880	51		
	52	Child tax credit. Attach Schedule 8812, if required	52		
	53	Residential energy credits. Attach Form 5695	53		
	54	Other credits from Form a ☐ 3800 b ☐ 8801 c ☐	54		
	55	Add lines 48 through 54. These are your total credits		55	
	56	Subtract line 55 from line 47. If line 55 is more than line 47, enter -0-	►	56	24,825
Other Taxes	57	Self-employment tax. Attach Schedule SE		57	9,902
	58	Unreported social security and Medicare tax from Form: a ☐ 4137 b ☐ 8919		58	
	59	Additional tax on IRAs, other qualified retirement plans, etc. Attach Form 5329 if required		59	
	60a	Household employment taxes from Schedule H		60a	
	b	First-time homebuyer credit repayment. Attach Form 5405 if required		60b	
	61	Health care: individual responsibility (see instructions) Full-year coverage ☒		61	
	62	Taxes from: a ☐ Form 8959 b ☐ Form 8960 c ☐ Instructions; enter code(s)		62	
	63	Add lines 56 through 62. This is your total tax	►	63	34,727
Payments	64	Federal income tax withheld from Forms W-2 and 1099	64	7,924	
If you have a qualifying child, attach Schedule EIC.	65	2016 estimated tax payments and amount applied from 2015 return	65		
	66a	Earned income credit (EIC)	66a		
	b	Nontaxable combat pay election	66b		
	67	Additional child tax credit. Attach Schedule 8812	67		
	68	American opportunity credit from Form 8863, line 8	68		
	69	Net premium tax credit. Attach Form 8962	69		
	70	Amount paid with request for extension to file	70		
	71	Excess social security and tier 1 RRTA tax withheld	71		
	72	Credit for federal tax on fuels. Attach Form 4136	72		
	73	Credits from Form: a ☐ 2439 b ☐ Reserved c ☐ 8885 d ☐	73		
	74	Add lines 64, 65, 66a, and 67 through 73. These are your total payments	►	74	7,924
Refund	75	If line 74 is more than line 63, subtract line 63 from line 74. This is the amount you overpaid		75	
	76a	Amount of line 75 you want refunded to you. If Form 8888 is attached, check here ► ☐		76a	
Direct deposit? See instructions.	► b	Routing number ____ ► c Type: ☐ Checking ☐ Savings			
	► d	Account number ____			
	77	Amount of line 75 you want applied to your 2017 estimated tax ►	77		
Amount You Owe	78	Amount you owe. Subtract line 74 from line 63. For details on how to pay, see instructions	►	78	26,959
	79	Estimated tax penalty (see instructions)	79	156	

Third Party Designee — Do you want to allow another person to discuss this return with the IRS (see instructions)? ☒ Yes. Complete below. ☐ No.
Designee's name ► ____ Phone no. ► ____ Personal identification number (PIN) ► 48059

Sign Here
Joint return? See instructions. Keep a copy for your records.
Your signature ____ Date ____ Your occupation **PROFESSOR** ____ Daytime phone number ____
Spouse's signature. If a joint return, both must sign. ____ Date ____ Spouse's occupation ____ If the IRS sent you an Identity Protection PIN, enter it here (see inst.) ____

Paid Preparer Use Only
Print/Type preparer's name: LEON BORODA | Preparer's signature: LEON BORODA | Date: 03/14/17 | Check ☐ if self-employed | PTIN: P00544949
Firm's name ► ____ | Firm's EIN ► 95-2848059
Firm's address ► ____ | Phone no. ____

www.irs.gov/form1040
DAA

Form **1040** (2016)

SCHEDULE C
(Form 1040)

Department of the Treasury
Internal Revenue Service   (99)

Profit or Loss From Business
(Sole Proprietorship)

▶ Information about Schedule C and its separate instructions is at *www.irs.gov/schedulec*.
▶ Attach to Form 1040, 1040NR, or 1041; partnerships generally must file Form 1065.

OMB No. 1545-0074

2016

Attachment
Sequence No. **09**

Name of proprietor

Social security number (SSN)

| A | Principal business or profession, including product or service (see instructions) | | B | Enter code from instructions ▶ |

| C | Business name. If no separate business name, leave blank. | | D | Employer ID number (EIN), (see instr.) |

| E | Business address (including suite or room no.) ▶ |
| | City, town or post office, state, and ZIP code |

| F | Accounting method: | (1) [X] Cash | (2) ☐ Accrual | (3) ☐ Other (specify) ▶ |

G	Did you "materially participate" in the operation of this business during 2016? If "No," see instructions for limit on losses	[X] Yes	☐ No
H	If you started or acquired this business during 2016, check here	▶ ☐
I	Did you make any payments in 2016 that would require you to file Form(s) 1099? (see instructions)	☐ Yes	[X] No
J	If "Yes," did you or will you file required Forms 1099?	☐ Yes	☐ No

Part I   Income

1	Gross receipts or sales. See instructions for line 1 and check the box if this income was reported to you on Form W-2 and the "Statutory employee" box on that form was checked	▶ ☐	1	121,236
2	Returns and allowances		2	
3	Subtract line 2 from line 1		3	121,236
4	Cost of goods sold (from line 42)		4	
5	Gross profit. Subtract line 4 from line 3		5	121,236
6	Other income, including federal and state gasoline or fuel tax credit or refund (see instructions)		6	
7	Gross income. Add lines 5 and 6	▶	7	121,236

Part II   Expenses. Enter expenses for business use of your home only on line 30.

8	Advertising	8		18	Office expense (see instructions)	18	2,691
9	Car and truck expenses (see instructions)	9	5,157	19	Pension and profit-sharing plans	19	
				20	Rent or lease (see instructions):		
10	Commissions and fees	10		a	Vehicles, machinery, and equipment	20a	7,714
11	Contract labor (see instructions)	11		b	Other business property	20b	15,416
12	Depletion	12		21	Repairs and maintenance	21	
13	Depreciation and section 179 expense deduction (not included in Part III) (see instructions)	13		22	Supplies (not included in Part III)	22	1,000
				23	Taxes and licenses	23	
				24	Travel, meals, and entertainment:		
14	Employee benefit programs (other than on line 19)	14		a	Travel	24a	12,325
15	Insurance (other than health)	15	206	b	Deductible meals and entertainment (see instructions)	24b	
16	Interest:			25	Utilities	25	
a	Mortgage (paid to banks, etc.)	16a		26	Wages (less employment credits)	26	
b	Other	16b		27a	Other expenses (from line 48)	27a	1,894
17	Legal and professional services	17	4,750	b	Reserved for future use	27b	

| 28 | Total expenses before expenses for business use of home. Add lines 8 through 27a | ▶ | 28 | 51,153 |
| 29 | Tentative profit or (loss). Subtract line 28 from line 7 | | 29 | 70,083 |
| 30 | Expenses for business use of your home. Do not report these expenses elsewhere. Attach Form 8829 unless using the simplified method (see instructions).
Simplified method filers only: enter the total square footage of: (a) your home _____ and (b) the part of your home used for business: _____. Use the Simplified Method Worksheet in the instructions to figure the amount to enter on line 30 | | 30 | |
| 31 | Net profit or (loss). Subtract line 30 from line 29.
• If a profit, enter on both Form 1040, line 12 (or Form 1040NR, line 13) and on Schedule SE, line 2. (If you checked the box on line 1, see instructions). Estates and trusts, enter on Form 1041, line 3.
• If a loss, you must go to line 32 | } | 31 | 70,083 |
| 32 | If you have a loss, check the box that describes your investment in this activity (see instructions).
• If you checked 32a, enter the loss on both Form 1040, line 12, (or Form 1040NR, line 13) and on Schedule SE, line 2. (If you checked the box on line 1, see the line 31 instructions). Estates and trusts, enter on Form 1041, line 3.
• If you checked 32b, you must attach Form 6198. Your loss may be limited. | } | 32a ☐ All investment is at risk.
32b ☐ Some investment is not at risk. |

For Paperwork Reduction Act Notice, see the separate instructions.
BAA

Schedule C (Form 1040) 2016

Part III Cost of Goods Sold (see instructions)

33 Method(s) used to value closing inventory: a ☐ Cost b ☐ Lower of cost or market c ☐ Other (attach explanation)

34 Was there any change in determining quantities, costs, or valuations between opening and closing inventory?
If "Yes," attach explanation .... ☐ Yes ☐ No

35	Inventory at beginning of year. If different from last year's closing inventory, attach explanation	35
36	Purchases less cost of items withdrawn for personal use	36
37	Cost of labor. Do not include any amounts paid to yourself	37
38	Materials and supplies	38
39	Other costs	39
40	Add lines 35 through 39	40
41	Inventory at end of year	41
42	Cost of goods sold. Subtract line 41 from line 40. Enter the result here and on line 4	42

Part IV Information on Your Vehicle. Complete this part only if you are claiming car or truck expenses on line 9 and are not required to file Form 4562 for this business. See the instructions for line 13 to find out if you must file Form 4562.

43 When did you place your vehicle in service for business purposes? (month, day, year) ▶ 01/01/15

44 Of the total number of miles you drove your vehicle during 2016, enter the number of miles you used your vehicle for:

a Business 8,000 b Commuting (see instructions) c Other 2,000

45	Was your vehicle available for personal use during off-duty hours?	☒ Yes	☐ No
46	Do you (or your spouse) have another vehicle available for personal use?	☒ Yes	☐ No
47a	Do you have evidence to support your deduction?	☐ Yes	☒ No
b	If "Yes," is the evidence written?	☐ Yes	☐ No

Part V Other Expenses. List below business expenses not included on lines 8-26 or line 30.

BUSINESS CELL PHONE	1,190
OFFICE TELEPHONE	420
EFAX	284

48	Total other expenses. Enter here and on line 27a	48	1,894

DAA Schedule C (Form 1040) 2016

SCHEDULE SE
(Form 1040)

Department of the Treasury
Internal Revenue Service   (99)

Self-Employment Tax

▶ Information about Schedule SE and its separate instructions is at www.irs.gov/schedulese.

▶ Attach to Form 1040 or Form 1040NR.

OMB No. 1545-0074

2016

Attachment
Sequence No. **17**

Name of person with **self-employment** income (as shown on Form 1040 or Form 1040NR)	Social security number of person with **self-employment** income ▶
▮▮▮▮▮▮	▮▮▮▮▮▮

Before you begin: To determine if you must file Schedule SE, see the instructions.

May I Use Short Schedule SE or Must I Use Long Schedule SE?

Note. Use this flowchart only if you must file Schedule SE. If unsure, see *Who Must File Schedule SE* in the instructions.

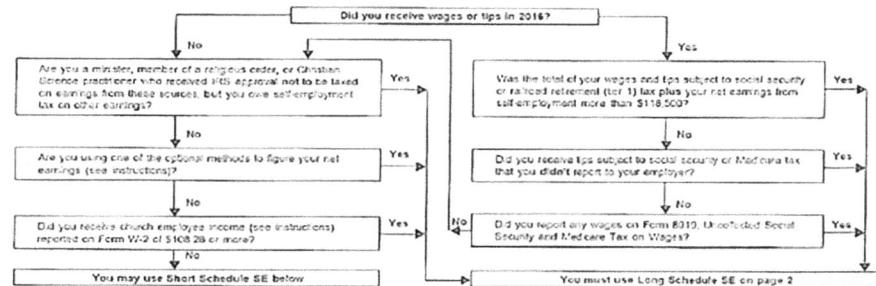

Section A — Short Schedule SE. Caution. Read above to see if you can use Short Schedule SE.

1a	Net farm profit or (loss) from Schedule F, line 34, and farm partnerships, Schedule K-1 (Form 1065), box 14, code A		1a	
b	If you received social security retirement or disability benefits, enter the amount of Conservation Reserve Program payments included on Schedule F, line 4b, or listed on Schedule K-1 (Form 1065), box 20, code Z		1b (	)
2	Net profit or (loss) from Schedule C, line 31; Schedule C-EZ, line 3; Schedule K-1 (Form 1065), box 14, code A (other than farming); and Schedule K-1 (Form 1065-B), box 9, code J1. Ministers and members of religious orders, see instructions for types of income to report on this line. See instructions for other income to report		2	70,083
3	Combine lines 1a, 1b, and 2		3	70,083
4	Multiply line 3 by 92.35% (0.9235). If less than $400, you don't owe self-employment tax; don't file this schedule unless you have an amount on line 1b	▶	4	64,722
	Note. If line 4 is less than $400 due to Conservation Reserve Program payments on line 1b, see instructions.			
5	Self-employment tax. If the amount on line 4 is:			
	• $118,500 or less, multiply line 4 by 15.3% (0.153). Enter the result here and on Form 1040, line 57, or Form 1040NR, line 55			
	• More than $118,500, multiply line 4 by 2.9% (0.029). Then, add $14,694 to the result. Enter the total here and on Form 1040, line 57, or Form 1040NR, line 55		5	9,902
6	Deduction for one-half of self-employment tax. Multiply line 5 by 50% (0.50). Enter the result here and on Form 1040, line 27, or Form 1040NR, line 27	6	4,951	

For Paperwork Reduction Act Notice, see your tax return instructions.

Schedule SE (Form 1040) 2016

DAA

Alternative Minimum Tax—Individuals

OMB No. 1545-0074

► Information about Form 6251 and its separate instructions is at *www.irs.gov/form6251.*

2016

Department of the Treasury
Internal Revenue Service   (99)

► Attach to Form 1040 or Form 1040NR.

Attachment
Sequence No. **32**

Name(s) shown on Form 1040 or Form 1040NR

Your social security number

	Part I	Alternative Minimum Taxable Income (See instructions for how to complete each line.)		
1	If filing Schedule A (Form 1040), enter the amount from Form 1040, line 41, and go to line 2. Otherwise, enter the amount from Form 1040, line 38, and go to line 7. (If less than zero, enter as a negative amount.)		1	127,930
2	Medical and dental. If you or your spouse was 65 or older, enter the smaller of Schedule A (Form 1040), line 4, or 2.5% (0.025) of Form 1040, line 38. If zero or less, enter -0-		2	
3	Taxes from Schedule A (Form 1040), line 9		3	
4	Enter the home mortgage interest adjustment, if any, from line 6 of the worksheet in the instructions for this line		4	
5	Miscellaneous deductions from Schedule A (Form 1040), line 27		5	
6	If Form 1040, line 38, is $155,650 or less, enter -0-. Otherwise, see instructions		6	( )
7	Tax refund from Form 1040, line 10 or line 21		7	( )
8	Investment interest expense (difference between regular tax and AMT)		8	
9	Depletion (difference between regular tax and AMT)		9	
10	Net operating loss deduction from Form 1040, line 21. Enter as a positive amount		10	
11	Alternative tax net operating loss deduction		11	( )
12	Interest from specified private activity bonds exempt from the regular tax		12	
13	Qualified small business stock, see instructions		13	
14	Exercise of incentive stock options (excess of AMT income over regular tax income)		14	
15	Estates and trusts (amount from Schedule K-1 (Form 1041), box 12, code A)		15	
16	Electing large partnerships (amount from Schedule K-1 (Form 1065-B), box 6)		16	
17	Disposition of property (difference between AMT and regular tax gain or loss)		17	
18	Depreciation on assets placed in service after 1986 (difference between regular tax and AMT)		18	
19	Passive activities (difference between AMT and regular tax income or loss)		19	
20	Loss limitations (difference between AMT and regular tax income or loss)		20	0
21	Circulation costs (difference between regular tax and AMT)		21	
22	Long-term contracts (difference between AMT and regular tax income)		22	
23	Mining costs (difference between regular tax and AMT)		23	
24	Research and experimental costs (difference between regular tax and AMT)		24	
25	Income from certain installment sales before January 1, 1987		25	( )
26	Intangible drilling costs preference		26	
27	Other adjustments, including income-based related adjustments		27	
28	Alternative minimum taxable income. Combine lines 1 through 27. (If married filing separately and line 28 is more than $247,450, see instructions.)		28	127,930

	Part II	Alternative Minimum Tax (AMT)			
29	Exemption. (If you were under age 24 at the end of 2016, see instructions.)				
	IF your filing status is . . .	AND line 28 is not over . . .	THEN enter on line 29 . . .		
	Single or head of household	$119,700	$53,900		
	Married filing jointly or qualifying widow(er)	159,700	83,800		
	Married filing separately	79,850	41,900		
	If line 28 is over the amount shown above for your filing status, see instructions.			29	51,842
30	Subtract line 29 from line 28. If more than zero, go to line 31. If zero or less, enter -0- here and on lines 31, 33, and 35, and go to line 34			30	76,088
31	• If you are filing Form 2555 or 2555-EZ, see instructions for the amount to enter. • If you reported capital gain distributions directly on Form 1040, line 13, you reported qualified dividends on Form 1040, line 9b, or you had a gain on both lines 15 and 16 of Schedule D (Form 1040) (as refigured for the AMT, if necessary), complete Part III on the back and enter the amount from line 64 here. • All others: If line 30 is $186,300 or less ($93,150 or less if married filing separately), multiply line 30 by 26% (0.26). Otherwise, multiply line 30 by 28% (0.28) and subtract $3,726 ($1,863 if married filing separately) from the result.			31	19,783
32	Alternative minimum tax foreign tax credit (see instructions)			32	
33	Tentative minimum tax. Subtract line 32 from line 31			33	19,783
34	Add Form 1040, line 44 (minus any tax from Form 4972), and Form 1040, line 46. Subtract from the result any foreign tax credit from Form 1040, line 48. If you used Schedule J to figure your tax on Form 1040, line 44, refigure that tax without using Schedule J before completing this line (see instructions)			34	24,825
35	AMT. Subtract line 34 from line 33. If zero or less, enter -0-. Enter here and on Form 1040, line 45			35	0

For Paperwork Reduction Act Notice, see your tax return instructions.

Form **6251** (2016)

DAA

Form **1120S**			**U.S. Income Tax Return for an S Corporation**						OMB No. 1545-0123
Department of the Treasury Internal Revenue Service			► Do not file this form unless the corporation has filed or is attaching Form 2553 to elect to be an S corporation. ► Go to www.irs.gov/Form1120S for instructions and the latest information.						**2017**

For calendar year 2017 or tax year beginning , ending

A S election effective date 01/01/17	TYPE	Name		D Employer Identification number
B Business activity code number (see instructions) 541600	OR	Number, street, and room or suite no. If a P.O. box, see instructions		E Date incorporated 02/03/2016
C Check if Sch. M-3 attached ☐	PRINT	City or town, state or province, country, and ZIP or foreign postal code		F Total assets (see instructions) $ 9,162

G Is the corporation electing to be an S corporation beginning with this tax year? ☒ Yes ☐ No If "Yes," attach Form 2553 if not already filed

H Check if (1) ☐ Final return (2) ☐ Name change (3) ☐ Address change (4) ☐ Amended return (5) ☐ S election termination or revocation

I Enter the number of shareholders who were shareholders during any part of the tax year ► 1

Caution: Include only trade or business income and expenses on lines 1a through 21. See the instructions for more information.

Income	1a Gross receipts or sales	1a	327,378	
	b Returns and allowances	1b		
	c Balance. Subtract line 1b from line 1a		1c	327,378
	2 Cost of goods sold (attach Form 1125-A)		2	
	3 Gross profit. Subtract line 2 from line 1c		3	327,378
	4 Net gain (loss) from Form 4797, line 17 (attach Form 4797)		4	
	5 Other income (loss) (see instructions—attach statement)		5	
	6 Total income (loss). Add lines 3 through 5 ►		6	327,378
Deductions (see instructions for limitations)	7 Compensation of officers (see instructions—attach Form 1125-E)		7	
	8 Salaries and wages (less employment credits)		8	
	9 Repairs and maintenance		9	
	10 Bad debts		10	
	11 Rents		11	
	12 Taxes and licenses		12	908
	13 Interest		13	
	14 Depreciation not claimed on Form 1125-A or elsewhere on return (attach Form 4562)		14	
	15 Depletion (Do not deduct oil and gas depletion.)		15	
	16 Advertising		16	
	17 Pension, profit-sharing, etc., plans		17	
	18 Employee benefit programs		18	
	19 Other deductions (attach statement) SEE STMT 1		19	33,633
	20 Total deductions. Add lines 7 through 19 ►		20	34,541
	21 Ordinary business income (loss). Subtract line 20 from line 6		21	292,837
Tax and Payments	22a Excess net passive income or LIFO recapture tax (see instructions)	22a		
	b Tax from Schedule D (Form 1120S)	22b		
	c Add lines 22a and 22b (see instructions for additional taxes)		22c	
	23a 2017 estimated tax payments and 2016 overpayment credited to 2017	23a		
	b Tax deposited with Form 7004	23b		
	c Credit for federal tax paid on fuels (attach Form 4136)	23c		
	d Add lines 23a through 23c		23d	
	24 Estimated tax penalty (see instructions). Check if Form 2220 is attached ► ☐		24	
	25 Amount owed. If line 23d is smaller than the total of lines 22c and 24, enter amount owed		25	
	26 Overpayment. If line 23d is larger than the total of lines 22c and 24, enter amount overpaid		26	
	27 Enter amount from line 26 Credited to 2018 estimated tax ► Refunded ►		27	

Sign Here	Under penalties of perjury, I declare that I have examined this return, including accompanying schedules and statements, and to the best of my knowledge and belief, it is true, correct, and complete. Declaration of preparer (other than taxpayer) is based on all information of which preparer has any knowledge.		May the IRS discuss this return with the preparer shown below (see instructions)? ☒ Yes ☐ No
►	Signature of officer	Date	Title PRESIDENT

Paid Preparer Use Only	Print/Type preparer's name	Preparer's signature	Date 04/14/18	Check ☐ if self-employed	PTIN P00544949
	Firm's name ►			Firm's EIN ►	
	Firm's address ►			Phone no.	

For Paperwork Reduction Act Notice, see separate instructions.

Form **1120S** (2017)

DAA

Schedule B   Other Information (see instructions)

		Yes	No
1	Check accounting method: a [X] Cash b [ ] Accrual c [ ] Other (specify) ▶		
2	See the instructions and enter the: a Business activity ▶ CONSULTING b Product or service ▶ CONSULTING		
3	At any time during the tax year, was any shareholder of the corporation a disregarded entity, a trust, an estate, or a nominee or similar person? If "Yes," attach Schedule B-1, Information on Certain Shareholders of an S Corporation		X
4	At the end of the tax year, did the corporation:		
a	Own directly 20% or more, or own, directly or indirectly, 50% or more of the total stock issued and outstanding of any foreign or domestic corporation? For rules of constructive ownership, see instructions. If "Yes," complete (i) through (v) below		X

(i) Name of Corporation	(ii) Employer Identification Number (if any)	(iii) Country of Incorporation	(iv) Percentage of Stock Owned	(v) If Percentage in (iv) is 100%, Enter the Date (if any) a Qualified Subchapter S Subsidiary Election Was Made

		Yes	No
b	Own directly an interest of 20% or more, or own, directly or indirectly, an interest of 50% or more in the profit, loss, or capital in any foreign or domestic partnership (including an entity treated as a partnership) or in the beneficial interest of a trust? For rules of constructive ownership, see instructions. If "Yes," complete (i) through (v) below		X

(i) Name of Entity	(ii) Employer Identification Number (if any)	(iii) Type of Entity	(iv) Country of Organization	(v) Maximum Percentage Owned in Profit, Loss, or Capital

		Yes	No
5a	At the end of the tax year, did the corporation have any outstanding shares of restricted stock?		X
	If "Yes," complete lines (i) and (ii) below.		
	(i) Total shares of restricted stock .... ▶		
	(ii) Total shares of non-restricted stock .... ▶		
b	At the end of the tax year, did the corporation have any outstanding stock options, warrants, or similar instruments?		X
	If "Yes," complete lines (i) and (ii) below.		
	(i) Total shares of stock outstanding at the end of the tax year .... ▶		
	(ii) Total shares of stock outstanding if all instruments were executed ...... ▶		
6	Has this corporation filed, or is it required to file, Form 8918, Material Advisor Disclosure Statement, to provide information on any reportable transaction?		X
7	Check this box if the corporation issued publicly offered debt instruments with original issue discount .... ▶ [ ]		
	If checked, the corporation may have to file Form 8281, Information Return for Publicly Offered Original Issue Discount Instruments.		
8	If the corporation: (a) was a C corporation before it elected to be an S corporation or the corporation acquired an asset with a basis determined by reference to the basis of the asset (or the basis of any other property) in the hands of a C corporation and (b) has net unrealized built-in gain in excess of the net recognized built-in gain from prior years, enter the net unrealized built-in gain reduced by net recognized built-in gain from prior years (see instructions) .... ▶ $		
9	Enter the accumulated earnings and profits of the corporation at the end of the tax year. .... $		
10	Does the corporation satisfy both of the following conditions?		
a	The corporation's total receipts (see instructions) for the tax year were less than $250,000		
b	The corporation's total assets at the end of the tax year were less than $250,000		X
	If "Yes," the corporation is not required to complete Schedules L and M-1.		
11	During the tax year, did the corporation have any non-shareholder debt that was canceled, was forgiven, or had the terms modified so as to reduce the principal amount of the debt?		X
	If "Yes," enter the amount of principal reduction .... $		
12	During the tax year, was a qualified subchapter S subsidiary election terminated or revoked? If "Yes," see instructions		X
13a	Did the corporation make any payments in 2017 that would require it to file Form(s) 1099?	X	
b	If "Yes," did the corporation file or will it file required Forms 1099?	X	

Form 1120S (2017)

DAA

Schedule K   Shareholders' Pro Rata Share Items

				Total amount
Income (Loss)	1	Ordinary business income (loss) (page 1, line 21)	1	292,837
	2	Net rental real estate income (loss) (attach Form 8825)	2	
	3a	Other gross rental income (loss)	3a	
	b	Expenses from other rental activities (attach statement)	3b	
	c	Other net rental income (loss). Subtract line 3b from line 3a	3c	
	4	Interest income	4	
	5	Dividends: a Ordinary dividends	5a	
		b Qualified dividends	5b	
	6	Royalties	6	
	7	Net short-term capital gain (loss) (attach Schedule D (Form 1120S))	7	
	8a	Net long-term capital gain (loss) (attach Schedule D (Form 1120S))	8a	
	b	Collectibles (28%) gain (loss)	8b	
	c	Unrecaptured section 1250 gain (attach statement)	8c	
	9	Net section 1231 gain (loss) (attach Form 4797)	9	
	10	Other income (loss) (see instructions) Type ▶	10	
Deductions	11	Section 179 deduction (attach Form 4562)	11	8,206
	12a	Charitable contributions SEE STMT 2	12a	1,000
	b	Investment interest expense	12b	
	c	Section 59(e)(2) expenditures (1) Type ▶ (2) Amount ▶	12c(2)	
	d	Other deductions (see instructions) Type ▶	12d	
Credits	13a	Low-income housing credit (section 42(j)(5))	13a	
	b	Low-income housing credit (other)	13b	
	c	Qualified rehabilitation expenditures (rental real estate) (attach Form 3468, if applicable)	13c	
	d	Other rental real estate credits (see instructions) Type ▶	13d	
	e	Other rental credits (see instructions) Type ▶	13e	
	f	Biofuel producer credit (attach Form 6478)	13f	
	g	Other credits (see instructions) Type ▶	13g	
Foreign Transactions	14a	Name of country or U.S. possession ▶		
	b	Gross income from all sources	14b	
	c	Gross income sourced at shareholder level	14c	
		Foreign gross income sourced at corporate level		
	d	Passive category	14d	
	e	General category	14e	
	f	Other (attach statement)	14f	
		Deductions allocated and apportioned at shareholder level		
	g	Interest expense	14g	
	h	Other	14h	
		Deductions allocated and apportioned at corporate level to foreign source income		
	i	Passive category	14i	
	j	General category	14j	
	k	Other (attach statement)	14k	
		Other information		
	l	Total foreign taxes (check one): ▶ ☐ Paid ☐ Accrued	14l	
	m	Reduction in taxes available for credit (attach statement)	14m	
	n	Other foreign tax information (attach statement)		
Alternative Minimum Tax (AMT) Items	15a	Post-1986 depreciation adjustment	15a	
	b	Adjusted gain or loss	15b	
	c	Depletion (other than oil and gas)	15c	
	d	Oil, gas, and geothermal properties – gross income	15d	
	e	Oil, gas, and geothermal properties – deductions	15e	
	f	Other AMT items (attach statement)	15f	
Items Affecting Shareholder Basis	16a	Tax-exempt interest income	16a	
	b	Other tax-exempt income	16b	
	c	Nondeductible expenses	16c	
	d	Distributions (attach statement if required) (see instructions)	16d	282,589
	e	Repayment of loans from shareholders	16e	

CAA

Schedule K	Shareholders' Pro Rata Share Items (continued)						Total amount
Other Information	17a	Investment income				17a	
	b	Investment expenses				17b	
	c	Dividend distributions paid from accumulated earnings and profits				17c	
	d	Other items and amounts (attach statement)					
Recon-ciliation	18	Income/loss reconciliation. Combine the amounts on lines 1 through 10 in the far right column. From the result, subtract the sum of the amounts on lines 11 through 12d and 14l				18	283,631

Schedule L	Balance Sheets per Books	Beginning of tax year				End of tax year	
	Assets	(a)		(b)		(c)	(d)
1	Cash						1,542
2a	Trade notes and accounts receivable						
b	Less allowance for bad debts	(		)		(	)
3	Inventories						
4	U.S. government obligations						
5	Tax-exempt securities (see instructions)						
6	Other current assets (attach statement)						
7	Loans to shareholders						
8	Mortgage and real estate loans						
9	Other investments (attach statement)						
10a	Buildings and other depreciable assets					8,206	
b	Less accumulated depreciation	(		)		(586	7,620
11a	Depletable assets						
b	Less accumulated depletion	(		)		(	)
12	Land (net of any amortization)						
13a	Intangible assets (amortizable only)						
b	Less accumulated amortization	(		)		(	)
14	Other assets (attach statement)						
15	Total assets			0			9,162
	Liabilities and Shareholders' Equity						
16	Accounts payable						
17	Mortgages, notes, bonds payable in less than 1 year						
18	Other current liabilities (attach statement)						
19	Loans from shareholders						
20	Mortgages, notes, bonds payable in 1 year or more						
21	Other liabilities (attach statement)						
22	Capital stock						500
23	Additional paid-in capital						
24	Retained earnings						8,662
25	Adjustments to shareholders' equity (attach statement)						( )
26	Less cost of treasury stock			(			( )
27	Total liabilities and shareholders' equity			0			9,162

OAA

Schedule M-1 Reconciliation of Income (Loss) per Books With Income (Loss) per Return

Note: The corporation may be required to file Schedule M-3 (see instructions)

1	Net income (loss) per books	291,251	5	Income recorded on books this year not included on Schedule K, lines 1 through 10 (itemize):	
2	Income included on Schedule K, lines 1, 2, 3c, 4, 5a, 6, 7, 8a, 9, and 10, not recorded on books this year (itemize)		a	Tax-exempt interest $	
3	Expenses recorded on books this year not included on Schedule K, lines 1 through 12 and 14l (itemize):		6	Deductions included on Schedule K, lines 1 through 12 and 14l, not charged against book income this year (itemize):	
a	Depreciation $		a	Depreciation $ 7,620	
b	Travel and entertainment $				7,620
			7	Add lines 5 and 6	7,620
4	Add lines 1 through 3	291,251	8	Income (loss) (Schedule K, line 18) Line 4 less line 7	283,631

Schedule M-2 Analysis of Accumulated Adjustments Account, Other Adjustments Account, and Shareholders' Undistributed Taxable Income Previously Taxed (see instructions)

		(a) Accumulated adjustments account	(b) Other adjustments account	(c) Shareholders' undistributed taxable income previously taxed
1	Balance at beginning of tax year			
2	Ordinary income from page 1, line 21	292,837		
3	Other additions			
4	Loss from page 1, line 21	(		
5	Other reductions STMT 3	9,206)		
6	Combine lines 1 through 5	283,631		
7	Distributions other than dividend distributions	282,589		
8	Balance at end of tax year Subtract line 7 from line 6	1,042		

Form **1120S** (2017)

DAA

671117
OMB No. 1545-0123

☐ Final K-1   ☐ Amended K-1

Schedule K-1	**2017**
(Form 1120S)	For calendar year 2017, or tax year
Department of the Treasury Internal Revenue Service	

beginning [   ]   ending [   ]

Shareholder's Share of Income, Deductions, Credits, etc.
▶ See back of form and separate instructions.

Part I	Information About the Corporation

A Corporation's employer identification number
81-1415824

B Corporation's name, address, city, state, and ZIP code

███████████████████████████

C IRS Center where corporation filed return
E-FILE

Part II	Information About the Shareholder

D Shareholder's identifying number
███████████

E Shareholder's name, address, city, state, and ZIP code

███████████████████████████

F Shareholder's percentage of stock ownership for tax year .... **100.000000** %

For IRS Use Only

Part III	Shareholder's Share of Current Year Income, Deductions, Credits, and Other Items

1	Ordinary business income (loss) **292,837**	13	Credits
2	Net rental real estate income (loss)		
3	Other net rental income (loss)		
4	Interest income		
5a	Ordinary dividends		
5b	Qualified dividends	14	Foreign transactions
6	Royalties		
7	Net short-term capital gain (loss)		
8a	Net long-term capital gain (loss)		
8b	Collectibles (28%) gain (loss)		
8c	Unrecaptured section 1250 gain		
9	Net section 1231 gain (loss)		
10	Other income (loss)	15	Alternative minimum tax (AMT) items
11	Section 179 deduction **8,206**	16 D	Items affecting shareholder basis **282,589**
12 A	Other deductions **1,000**		
		17	Other information

* See attached statement for additional information.

For Paperwork Reduction Act Notice, see the Instructions for Form 1120S.   www.irs.gov/Form1120S   Schedule K-1 (Form 1120S) 2017

DAA

Form **4562**

Department of the Treasury
Internal Revenue Service   (99)

Depreciation and Amortization
(Including Information on Listed Property)
▶ Attach to your tax return.
▶ Go to www.irs.gov/Form4562 for instructions and the latest information.

OMB No. 1545-0172

2017

Attachment
Sequence No. **179**

Name(s) shown on return ▮▮▮▮▮▮▮▮▮▮   Identifying number ▮▮▮▮▮▮

Business or activity to which this form relates
REGULAR DEPRECIATION

Part I Election To Expense Certain Property Under Section 179
Note: If you have any listed property, complete Part V before you complete Part I.

1	Maximum amount (see instructions)			1	510,000
2	Total cost of section 179 property placed in service (see instructions)			2	8,206
3	Threshold cost of section 179 property before reduction in limitation (see instructions)			3	2,030,000
4	Reduction in limitation. Subtract line 3 from line 2. If zero or less, enter -0-			4	0
5	Dollar limitation for tax year. Subtract line 4 from line 1. If zero or less, enter -0-. If married filing separately, see instructions			5	510,000

6	(a) Description of property	(b) Cost (business use only)	(c) Elected cost
	FURNITURE & FIXTURES	8,206	8,206

7	Listed property. Enter the amount from line 29		7		
8	Total elected cost of section 179 property. Add amounts in column (c), lines 6 and 7			8	8,206
9	Tentative deduction. Enter the smaller of line 5 or line 8			9	8,206
10	Carryover of disallowed deduction from line 13 of your 2016 Form 4562			10	
11	Business income limitation. Enter the smaller of business income (not less than zero) or line 5 (see instructions)			11	292,837
12	Section 179 expense deduction. Add lines 9 and 10, but don't enter more than line 11			12	8,206
13	Carryover of disallowed deduction to 2018. Add lines 9 and 10, less line 12	▶	13		

Note: Don't use Part II or Part III below for listed property. Instead, use Part V.

Part II Special Depreciation Allowance and Other Depreciation (Don't include listed property.) (See instructions.)

14	Special depreciation allowance for qualified property (other than listed property) placed in service during the tax year (see instructions)	14	
15	Property subject to section 168(f)(1) election	15	
16	Other depreciation (including ACRS)	16	

Part III MACRS Depreciation (Don't include listed property.) (See instructions.)

Section A

17	MACRS deductions for assets placed in service in tax years beginning before 2017	17	0
18	If you are electing to group any assets placed in service during the tax year into one or more general asset accounts, check here ▶ ☐		

Section B—Assets Placed in Service During 2017 Tax Year Using the General Depreciation System

(a) Classification of property	(b) Month and year placed in service	(c) Basis for depreciation (business/investment use only—see instructions)	(d) Recovery period	(e) Convention	(f) Method	(g) Depreciation deduction
19a 3-year property						
b 5-year property						
c 7-year property						
d 10-year property						
e 15-year property						
f 20-year property						
g 25-year property			25 yrs.		S/L	
h Residential rental property			27.5 yrs.	MM	S/L	
			27.5 yrs.	MM	S/L	
i Nonresidential real property			39 yrs.	MM	S/L	
				MM	S/L	

Section C—Assets Placed in Service During 2017 Tax Year Using the Alternative Depreciation System

20a Class life					S/L	
b 12-year			12 yrs.		S/L	
c 40-year			40 yrs.	MM	S/L	

Part IV Summary (See instructions.)

21	Listed property. Enter amount from line 28	21	
22	Total. Add amounts from line 12, lines 14 through 17, lines 19 and 20 in column (g), and line 21. Enter here and on the appropriate lines of your return. Partnerships and S corporations—see instructions	22	
23	For assets shown above and placed in service during the current year, enter the portion of the basis attributable to section 263A costs	23	

For Paperwork Reduction Act Notice, see separate instructions.

EM

Form **4562** (2017)

THERE ARE NO AMOUNTS FOR PAGE 2

ABOUT THE AUTHOR

Brian D. Lerner is an Immigration Lawyer and runs a National Immigration Law Firm for nearly 30 years. He is an attorney who is a certified specialist that might help in Immigration & Nationality Law as issued by the California State Bar, Board of Legal Specialization. Attorney Lerner is an expert in Immigration Law, Removal and Deportation, Citizenship, Waiver and Appeals.

He has been a licensed attorney since 1992 and started the Law Offices of Brian D. Lerner, APC. The immigration practice consists of Immigration and Nationality Law, and everything involved with and regarding immigration which includes citizenship, investment visas, family and employment visas, removal and deportation hearings, appeals, waivers, adjustment, consulate processing and all types of immigration and citizenship matters.

He has represented clients from all over the U.S. and in many countries around the world. One side of his practice is dedicated to keeping people in the U.S. and fighting for their immigration rights, while another side is to get people back who have been deported and removed from the U.S.

Also, there is the affirmative part of Immigration Law which Brian Lerner has helped numerous people come into the U.S. on business visas, investment visas, student visas, fiancée and marriage visas, religious visas and many more. Attorney Lerner has helped immigrants who are victims of crime and domestic violence or ones that are married to abusers.

In other words, Attorney Lerner has a firm that helps people all over the U.S. He has dedicated significant time to preparing numerous petitions and applications for you to get at a fraction of the price of hiring an attorney. He says it is the next best thing to a real attorney because they are real petitions prepared by an expert.

www.ingramcontent.com/pod-product-compliance
Lightning Source LLC
Chambersburg PA
CBHW060927210326
41597CB00042B/4641